This book belongs to:

{ _____ }

The Bible is God's special book and it teaches us that a long time ago God made the sun, the moon, the stars, and the whole world.

In the world God planted a beautiful garden. He filled the garden with plants and trees and animals.

He then made the first two people, Adam and Eve, and He put them in the garden too. They had everything they needed, and they spent time with God in the garden every day.

Life was perfect for them. Do you see how happy they look?

God is the Cloud. That's how He looks sometimes. See, He's with Adam and Eve in the garden.

Adam and Eve could enjoy everything in the garden: the animals, the trees, and most importantly, being with God.

There was only one rule, they couldn't eat of the tree of the knowledge of good and evil.

God knew that tree's fruit was bad for them, and if they ate its fruit they would die.

God tried to protect them, so God warned Adam and Eve not to eat from that tree.

It's like when your mommy and daddy tell you not to play in the street or jump on your bed. They want to protect you and keep you safe.

But just like you don't always listen to your mommy and daddy, Adam and Eve didn't listen to God, and they ate the bad fruit.

God was very sad. Adam and Eve had to leave the garden. They couldn't be with the animals or the trees, but worst of all, they couldn't be with God.

They left the garden, and just like God said, eventually they died.

God felt very sad because He loved Adam and Eve very much. God wanted to be with them in the garden forever.

Adam and Eve had lots of children before they died, and soon people filled the whole world.

Some of these people loved God and tried to do what He said, just like you love your parents and try to do what they say. But even the people who loved God the most weren't good all the time.

Other people didn't care about God and did whatever they wanted.

God saw this and loved them all anyway. But He couldn't be close to them because of the bad things they did.

These bad things are called "sins". Everyone sinned and would eventually have to die because of their sins, just like Adam and Eve did.

Imagine you're wearing a white shirt and you get dirt on it. Just like your parents want you to keep your shirt clean, God wants you to keep your heart clean.

A sin is like a dirty spot on your clean shirt. Sins make dirty spots on your heart. God never sins, He is perfect and always loving.

God is so good that our hearts must be totally clean if we want to be with Him like Adam and Eve were in the garden.

The Bible tells us that there is nobody who has a perfectly clean heart, not even one single person.

Look at the people in the picture. The dirty spots on their clothing are like the sin spots on their hearts.

Like them, we all have sin spots on our hearts that separate us from God.

Heaven is God's home high above the world. He lives there with His Son - Jesus. God wanted to be with us very much, but He couldn't because of the sin spots on our hearts.

Jesus loves us too, so They made a plan to save everyone from their sins, even you and me.

In Their plan Jesus would come to the world as a baby boy. He would never do anything bad so His heart would stay perfectly clean.

Jesus would then take ALL of OUR sin spots onto His heart. Then He would die (like Adam and Eve) and be separated from God. Then God would raise Him from the dead.

God and Jesus love us so much that They made this plan to save us from our sins so we can be with Them forever.

Jesus came into the world as a baby boy and He kept His heart clean.

Just like it's not always easy for us to be good, it wasn't easy for Jesus either.

Jesus went through everything we do, but He still kept His heart clean because He was here to save us.

Jesus also read the parts of the Bible that were already written so that He could teach us about God while He was here.

Jesus showed the people how much God loves them by healing all their boo-boos and teaching them about God.

Jesus wants us to get closer to God because that is how we can have our best possible lives.

Jesus loves us and wants the best for us, so He is always working to bring us closer to God.

The time came for God and Jesus to finish Their plan. Jesus lived a perfect life and kept His heart totally clean.

Some bad people put Jesus on a cross and killed him.

They didn't understand that Jesus wanted to help them. But this was all part of the plan. When Jesus died, He took all of the sin spots that we would ever have onto His heart.

Then God had to separate Himself from Jesus the same way He separated Himself from Adam and Eve. This was a terrible punishment for Jesus to be separated from God, but Jesus went through it for us.

Jesus took all of the punishment for sins that would ever have to be given. Jesus took all of our sins and all of the punishment so we can have clean hearts and be with God forever.

Even though God was sad that Jesus had to die, He was also very happy because Jesus had finished Their plan.

After three days God brought Jesus back to life. Jesus spent time in the world with His friends, and then God took Jesus back to Heaven.

God was so pleased that He made Jesus the King and Lord over everything.

So Jesus saved us, and Jesus is our Lord. That is why we say "Jesus is my Lord and Savior".

We all have sin spots on our hearts, but Jesus can give us a clean heart. We don't have to be separated from God like Adam and Eve, we can be with God forever.

Jesus died to save us from our sins, and we call this "salvation." Salvation is a gift from God, the best gift anyone could ever give.

To receive salvation we must believe that Jesus died for us and God brought Him back to life, and we must declare that Jesus is the Lord of our lives.

(Remember, Jesus is your Lord and Savior.) God then takes away our sin spots and makes our hearts clean.

God and Jesus even come to live in our hearts so we can be together right now and forever.

We can't see Jesus and God like you see them in this picture, but they are right here with us all the time.

Just like Jesus we should read the Bible to learn about God, and now our Bible includes stories about Jesus too.

We should also go to church to learn all we can about God and Jesus and to make friends with others who love Jesus.

Jesus also said we should tell others about Him so He can be their Lord and Savior too.

God has a wonderful plan for your life and it starts when you accept Jesus as your Lord and Savior. Are you ready? All you have to do is pray this prayer -

"Dear God, thank you for sending your Son Jesus to save me. I believe that He died for my sins and that you made Him alive again on the third day. I'm sorry for my sins and I will always try to listen to you. Please forgive me and give me a clean heart. Jesus is my Lord and Savior. Thank you that I now have a relationship with you and Jesus that will last forever. In Jesus' Name I pray, amen."

If you prayed that prayer then Jesus is your Lord and Savior, your heart is clean and God and Jesus have come to live in your heart. They will lead you and help you and be with you forever. Just like They made a plan to save you, They have many other great plans for your life. Remember to talk to Them and read your Bible. They are always with you, and They will never stop loving you.

Jesus is my Lord and Savior

Written by: Byron Howell
Illustrated by: Anja Sutton

Acknowledgements

Byron and Anja would like to jointly dedicate this book to Evangelist Eric Gonyon. We pray that all of God's people would have your heart for sharing the Gospel of Jesus Christ.

Anja Sutton

"O LORD, You are my God; I will exalt You, I will praise and give thanks to Your name; For you have done miraculous things, Plans formed long, long ago, [fulfilled] with perfect faithfulness."(Isaiah 25:1, AMP)

Special thanks to Byron Howell for an opportunity of a lifetime.

Byron Howell

"My child, listen to me and do as I say, and you will have a long, good life. I will teach you wisdom's ways and lead you in straight paths. When you walk, you won't be held back; when you run, you won't stumble. Take hold of my instructions; don't let them go. Guard them, for they are the key to life." (Proverbs 4:10-13, NLT)

Special thanks to my mother and father, there was never a doubt about our God.
Special thanks to my amazing wife and daughters, truly wonderful gifts from God.

ISBN: 978-0-578-18942-0

www.ExploitsforGod.com
Cover Design & Book Formatted by: Elijah Blyden, Sr.
Category: Christian Children's Book
Printed in the United States of America